EMMA

LOVE POEMS

SOMDEV CHATTOPADHYAY

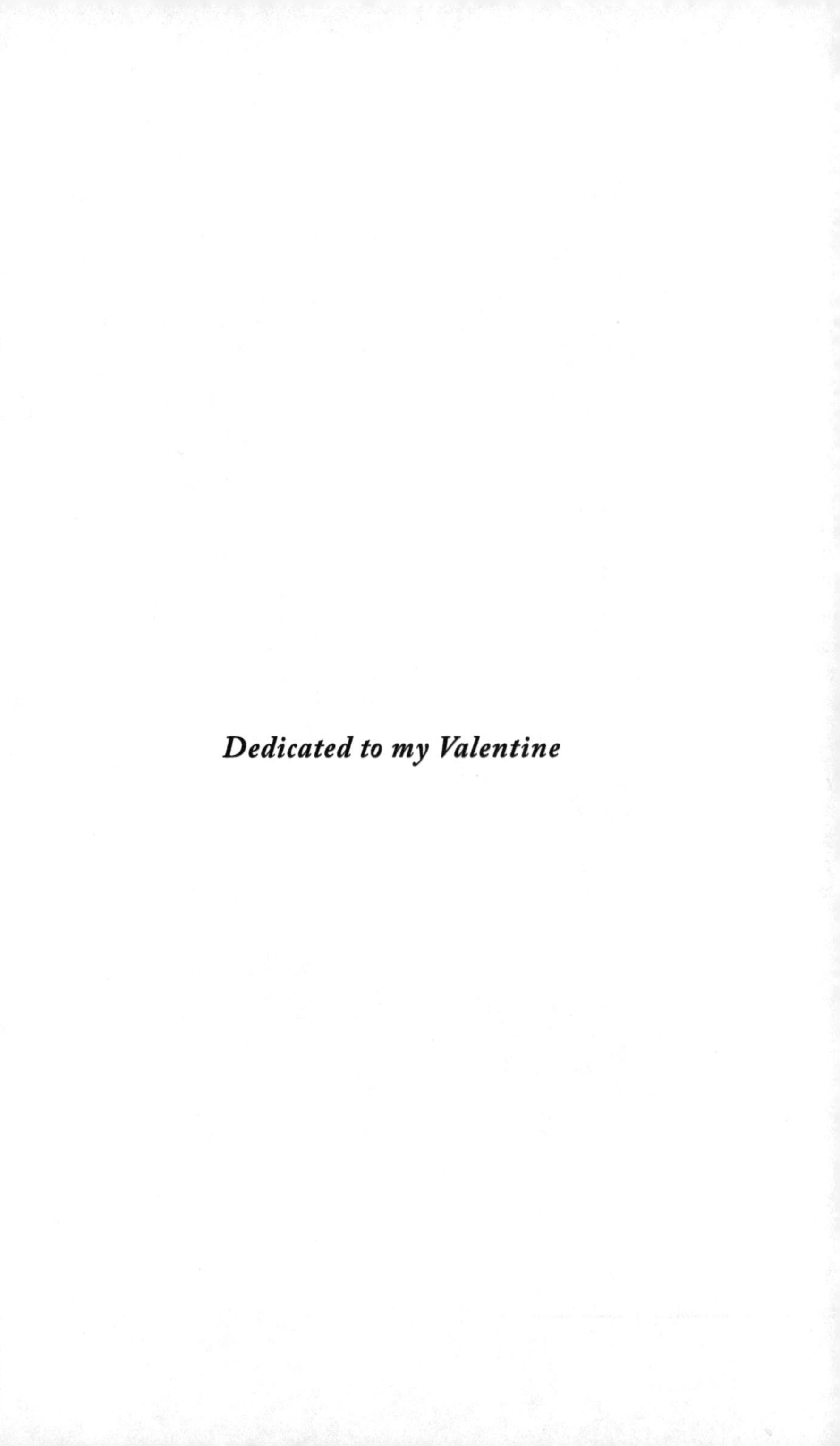

Dedicated to my Valentine

Contents

Preface — vii

Acknowledgements — ix

1. The Winter Bird — 1

2. I Am Not Afraid — 2

3. I Love Fire — 3

4. Emma Is A River — 4

5. The Sky Is Flying — 5

6. A Woman With A Poet — 6

7. I Gave Her Name After The Rain — 7

8. The Relationship — 8

9. It Doesn't Rain — 9

10. Waiting On The Border — 10

11. It All Changed — 11

12. Good Girl Bad Girl — 12

13. Terror And Love — 13

14. Now Is The Time Of Youth In Poetry — 14

15. From The Pretty Shillong Peak — 15

16. Where Are You, Emma? — 16

17. Love That I Wanted — 17

18. Sickness — 19

19. There Is Still Someone — 20

20. Emma At That Noon — 21

21. You Are Only Afraid — 22

22. Even If You Don't Agree With Me — 23

Contents

23. Fullmoon Night Again   24

24. Questions To Emma   25

25. Fear And Love   26

26. Sorry!   27

27. For You, Emma   28

28. I Do Not Want To Be Surprised   29

29. In The Valley   30

30. You And Emma   31

Preface

Valentine's Day is one of the most special days for people who are in love. The month of February is known as the month of valentine's gives us an opportunity to declare our love for special ones in front of the world and make them feel special.

Acknowledgements

My lovely friends

1. The winter bird

You were waiting throughout the morning
Might be lonely at noon and in the afternoon
With blurred eyes
You were searching for the winter birds
You might have jumped from the roof wall
And got some serious injuries
Country ships would come
And mast downstairs
You would wear a white shell necklace
And thousands of pearls and
Red corals would salute you, Emma, my dear!
Perhaps, you are imagining such
and getting wet alone in the falling snow
I have all of your sorrows with me
And about your Christmas gifts?
I have taken out the only bluebird
I had in my heart
Take this as your winter bird …
I just have flown it for you, Emma, O my dear!

2. I am not afraid

If I have so much courage, why am I afraid?
That is like that cowardly firefly
Here and there, the excluded, scattered light points
Do you know the reason?
This bio-luminescence of the cowardly firefly is actually
A youth's determination to revolt
One of the inevitable attractions in the game of light,
To transcend is almost impossible
The wild partridge knows, the tribal girl knows,
Knows the deep forest
The evening knows, the hills and grasslands,
The wind knows, the rain knows
And a woman firefly knows the best
Does anyone else know that?

3. I love fire

I love fire to burn and to be burnt alive
This is a well-known fact ... love causes burnt wounds
and sleepless nights
Someone's lost flute is taken care of
by someone who loves somewhere
The rest of the youth is still alive in your eyes
On the open back of the full moon
I still feel overwhelmed, still scattered at night
Whether you do love or not searching for fire,
I roam on the riverside
I never want to burn your home
Stand still in suspicion
Keep some acting stored
Nobody knows ... when the rebellion starts as such
For sure, I still love fire very much

4. Emma is a river

O independent State, O civilized life
you give my river Emma back
Her desire, her love ... let me touch once
I have seen the orphaned childhood
for a long time,
I saw deception and crafty kinship,
the penniless, lonely student life
I understood the sex and forbidden nights,
the numerous political sins of wounded society,
the hunter is swift as lightning,
and the clever crime
I saw the misery of exploited and failed women
I have been carrying, the distorted,
the dead body of the firm truth for a time
I'm almost exhausted, almost zero
It seems, at last, a person likes to go back
to where he started life
O Goddess, return the childhood of my father,
who prematurely died
Give me the unseen village back and
the beautiful river Emma which flows beside

5. The sky is flying

This time, I saw her as a sunshine
The entire summer came down in the city
I snatched the tearing trade kite ...
The sky is now flying in the night

6. A woman with a poet

I dreamed last night … Emma, you became a woman
I was restless the whole night
I decided to take you with me to the auditorium
As I will be taking part in a poetry reading event
So that after listening to the poetry,
you may become a real woman
I will see you with my heart and soul
Your lips, breast line, or wherever you say
I will go there with mica grains
Then there is no reason,
why you would not become a woman!
Actually, I am the poet who touched the poem
with the last night's red rose-stained dream
so that you may become a little more woman
Keeping my head in your lap and
taking the smell of spring
Even I may become a little more poet then!

7. I gave her name after the rain

Today is my long-awaited happiness
The happiness is in the rain
The smell of coitus in my body ...
I want to run ... run away
Ah! My earth is getting wet
Wet blood, wet many body sweats ...
The opportunists, money,
exploited women, and ammunition
Ah! Let it all soak
I have seen a lot of greedy faces
Just got what I didn't want
Let all the burning cords of my body be taken out
Today is the rain of happiness all night
A holy monk walks on the path of the rain
The child who is born today
I gave her name after the rain

8. The relationship

I rejected your utterly ignorant request

with lily flowers in hand

Don't you know the age,

when the arrow of romance stabs the heart?

Numerous white cows, sheep, and horses

in the endless green valley, circle around you

Like many untoward relationships,

numerous butterflies come for your love

The shame of bathing in Pangthumai falls alone

The clear water bed of sinking stone

Let the lily flowers be the reflected lips reservoir

Let me become skilled and flow in love.

In the full moonlight, snow is just accumulating

Let the December come in the river Piyain

My dear Emma, please wait for a while ...

The relationship is not quite brave and self-reliant!

9. It doesn't rain

If it rained, Emma would become
Soft like blackberries
But now it doesn't rain
Not even in length
Sometimes I shout and hurt
So that she bursts into tears
If firefly takes, it's raining
And decorate her with its light!

10. Waiting on the border

It is yet not let, please don't count your bullet
You may kiss me on the forehead once and forever
Emma, I am still waiting on the border
Can't we forget bullets and gunpowder?

11. It all changed

The houses are all changed,
life is like a punctuation mark
Why do you worry my Emma!
Turning the dusty leaves upside down,
To whom do you search so much?
Parents, property, the way, the need is all changed
In the right balance of investment,
I also have changed a lot
But know that still in my life,
the cloudy afternoon comes and
your image reflects in my eyes
I know, I know that you will say now,
the houses are all changed,
life is like a punctuation mark ...!

12. Good girl Bad girl

I saw Emma like a wax constantly melting
They told you, you're bad
Because you got the only man, you wanted wholeheartedly
They just told you,
They wanted a mild touch of your blue vein
I saw you constantly flowing like the solitary river
They told you, 'emigrate'.
Because you heard a single man continuously ...
Byron, Shelly, Keats, and Wordsworth
In fact, they wanted to feel the glory of western love
I saw you like a disobedient distracted in an untimely rain.
Yes, you did a wrong job,
You believed in a traitor for a long time
Those who say, Emma is bad, don't know that love is a belief
That up to the horizon, you are a really good girl

13. Terror and love

To touch the aircraft wheel on the country's soil
An emergency message ...
Authorities have arranged for drinking, feeding, and sleeping
Emergency and sudden landing of soldiers across the country ...
After seventy two hours of terrorism,
I came to know I lost my dearest Nicholas
With the twin towers, the pride of the nation
I lost him forever
After the catastrophe, with frightened and terrified hands,
I opened the letterbox one day
A sealed blue envelope was delivered, stamped on 2001/09/11
The pearls are shed by him ...
"My dear Emma, you're my love .... and beyond love "

14. Now is the time of youth in poetry

I saw you in your poetry
A bunch of orchid baths in solitary forests
In your writings …
The odd smell of water drops in the wet breast line of the hill
I saw youth in your poetry
You never wanted a separate state
But some want to be isolated
Now you are young
Go ahead, bathe in heavy rain
Then build resistance
Now is the time of youth in poetry
My dream of a common world
The water, the ground, the sky altogether
I believe youth is one name of life
I saw youth in your poetry
And I saw youth in your life

15. From the pretty Shillong peak

Day curfew throughout the city
The cavalry, which went on this route, is missing
And the falling fog nearly wiped their footprints
In the full moon night, the hills become a silver canvas
And Emma likes to go missing on this way
Facing the pretty Shillong peak, I am sitting up
Oh space, enlighten human life!
The seven stars of the Ursa Major can never be separated

16. Where are you, Emma?

Where did you go, last December in voluntary exile?
Somewhere, a man was waiting for you!
Now, deep in my mind, there is something without my
knowledge
Is love like an unruly fog?
If someone looks at you even for a moment, I become jealous of it
The day you distributed thousands of clothes and food in remote
villages
And a group of orphaned children clung to your tigress-like waist
Even that day I was jealous!
Even at this age, for no reason, like a mad,
I want to lay my head on your chest and see the ocean and sky
How wide is the scope of your embrace, I want to know
Why did you leave me again? Did you desire that I beg you?
Well, here I am turning away
If someone touches you, I will never get angry anymore
Will never ask again, Emma, where you are?

17. Love that I wanted

That is the unbelievable love I wanted!
That is the unrequited love I wanted!
Amid thousands of pandemics and epidemics
you did never leave me
In heavy rain, drought, and volcanic eruptions
even in strong earthquakes, you were steadfast forever
You never told anyone,
Keep your mouth shut! Listen to me you arrogant!
You never persuaded someone to become a poet
Yet, in all countries of the world, in all languages,
there are millions of poems only about you
Even in hundreds of ridicules or insults,
you did never leave me
All the dirt off my mind and all the false accusations,
you are the one who wiped carefully
though your clothes became torn and dirtier
Yet you never ever said,
that you also had some needs
Yet, in a dark poor cottage
in the midst of fragmented light
in your timid, sad watery eyes
I could see the poorness of this world

That is the unconditional love I wanted!
That is the mesmerizing love I wanted!
Every time one dies in this town, village,
or anywhere else, you have found yourself guilty
But those who could but never care
why someone dies of hunger or fear!
who is actually responsible for a death?
Still,
I wanted to live innumerable times at your touch
in the heart of this burnt country,
I wanted to be born again and again just for you
In any struggle, in any failure, you did never leave me
For every human being
From you,
That is the unbelievable love I wanted!
That is the unrequited love I wanted!

18. Sickness

It was the coming afternoon
Emma said, today I will pat your head a little!
But I forbade!
Resting head on her thigh like a dream
I was looking at the valley and clouds
And the bright mountains and bright sunlight for so long
A star was born from the Neonatal fever
A visible ring formed, radiating from her lap
The star touched the beach and settled in the sky
But then evening did not come at all
I begged Emma to give birth to stars
And said, when a star is sick, put your hand on its head
The way all the mothers did for years

19. There is still someone

That's why you suddenly look for someone
That's why I want to live to say this,
one day you will make some sweets for me
That's why it shines like the autumn sky
It seems, there is still someone!
But the moments spent together, I couldn't count
We did not meet again at the last book fair
It was almost as if we had never seen each other
But just before going to sleep
I feel you touch me for a moment
Even in this turbulent pandemic
Your eyes wake up for me and shine
I feel, Yes! there is still someone
The sorrow of not getting a thousand letters is gone

20. Emma at that noon

Seeing the butterfly in her hair, I understood,
Emma would come to the garret at noon,
unorganized and messy in her style and spell
A cloud would suddenly be transmitted
And there would be a sudden rain fall
I would make a picture with pieces of dream glass
Seeing Emma in private at that noon
I thought her roaring forty and me a colorful pebble

21. You are only afraid

You know how to love
Know how to laugh at happy words
You only fear the city!
You can love
For someone else
You are still afraid of the truth!

22. Even if you don't agree with me

Your eyes are all full of tears
But do you think
You are the only one to know how to cry!
My eyes are also full of tears
that can wet you in a dusty field
Even if you don't agree with me

23. Fullmoon night again

During the last full moons,
the moonlight did not come to my alley
Tonight is also a full moon
And I am again standing in the alley
What is love even tonight?

24. Questions to Emma

[1]

You see the day, I am the sleepless night

I stay always near you

Then why didn't it rain in Cox's Bazar?

[2]

I'm still standing in your yard

It's heavily raining today

Won't you tell me to come in dear?

25. Fear and Love

[1]

Everything I have given is a sacrifice

But I stay a while

Because I fear

If someone asks,

'Why do you call me so many times?'

[2]

No one remembers

But she called me, 'O Dear'!

Some say that's a cheating

No one remembers

But I call it her love

26. Sorry!

Alas, if I had trusted God a little more!
If I could hold Emma's hands twice
Perhaps, someone's friendship would turn into love
Perhaps, life could handle me a little more
The boat might be in the river
But I could sail to get the edge on the side
Sorry, if I had trusted myself a little more!

27. For you, Emma

A fall afternoon makes winter so cloudy
It absorbs all the fragrance
Endless fog drenches white rose
I really had nothing to offer you
Ignore this poverty
Emma, I beg a world of whiteness for you

28. I do not want to be surprised

When you like the writings of all other poets
I'm not surprised
Sitting beside a restless river, you stay calm and quiet
I'm not surprised
Even if countless rose buds sprout in your garden
I'm not surprised
But how you hold all the pain in your heart for ages
I am very surprised
But that I never want to be!

29. In the valley

A hawk is coming down from above in the valley
There seems to be a burning smell somewhere
Some people have blood stains on their lips
I can see a teenage girl walking alone
It's dark out there, and she's alone
In the valley now the tribals cheer
It seems someone is to be taken with both hands tied
Who is saying, I want to sacrifice tonight!
It's so dark here, and we're all alone
But I can clearly see the predatory claws
And many blood stains!
I can hear wild birds screeching
Wanting to run away somewhere, everywhere chill traps
Fire is on one side
And there is a deep ditch on the other
And that girl is walking right there
Maybe these are mere words
No one touched his clothes
But still, I fear
If those helpless eyes are not sheltered somehow
And if she suddenly asks, Emma, you too!

30. You and Emma

You are familiar with me but sometimes,
it seems that this is my first acquaintance!
Sometimes it seems I have never seen you before,
you are never mine!
But whenever you sprinkle olive leaves all over me
Wipe away all painful winter wounds with a caress
I find your amazing similarity with Emma!